KU-694-941

Fact Finders®

Theme Park Science

# MOTION at the THEME PARK

by Tammy Enz

a Capstone company — publishers for children

Raintree is an imprint of Capstone Global Library Limited, a company incorporated in England and Wales having its registered office at 264 Banbury Road, Oxford, OX2 7DY – Registered company number: 6695582

www.raintree.co.uk
myorders@raintree.co.uk



Edited by Carrie Braulick Sheely
Designed by Tracy McCabe
Original illustrations © Capstone Global Library Limited 2020
Picture research by Eric Gohl
Production by Kathy McColley
Originated by Capstone Global Library Ltd
Printed and bound in India

978 1 4747 8513 6 (hardback)
978 1 4747 8517 4 (paperback)

**British Library Cataloguing in Publication Data**
A full catalogue record for this book is available from the British Library.

**Acknowledgements**
We would like to thank the following for permission to reproduce photographs: Alamy: Skip Caplan, 12; iStockphoto: briannolan, 23, CasarsaGuru, 19, 25, Photomick, 27, tacojim, 13; Newscom/ZUMA Press: Kyle Grantham, 11, Sam Gangwer, 9; Shutterstock: ChameleonsEye, back cover (background), 1 (background), 15, Chris Howey, 17, Doug Lemke, 7, George Sheldon, 29, I Wei Huang, 16, Krylovochka, cover (bottom), 1 (bottom), Maria Bell, 5, Shooting Star Studio, 21; SuperStock: agf photo, cover (top). Design elements: Shutterstock.

# CONTENTS

CHAPTER 1

# MOTION RULES!



Spinning. Looping. Swinging. Dropping! Wherever you look in the theme park, you'll see motion. Motion is the key to non-stop thrills and stomach-dropping fun. It keeps you looping on the roller coaster, spinning on the Waltzers and crashing in the bumper cars.

Motion simply means movement. All the head-spinning, eye-popping motion at a theme park might seem random and out of control. But motion follows the laws of **physics**.

Do you want to see how the laws of motion work? Strap yourself in for a wild ride, and let's get moving!

**physics** study of matter and energy, including light, heat, electricity and motion

As the drop tower ride speeds downwards, it can reach 100 km (60 miles) per hour.

**FACT:**

In 2017, the top 25 theme parks in the world had 244 million visitors.

# The Laws of Motion

All motion follows the same rules. Famous scientist Sir Isaac Newton studied and defined the rules of motion more than 300 years ago. Newton's three laws are:

1. Objects that are moving keep moving without changing direction. Objects that aren't moving stay still. A force must act on an object to change its motion. A force is a pushing or pulling action. Newton's first law is also called the law of **inertia**.

2. The change in an object's motion depends on its **mass** and the strength of force applied to it. The mass of an object is all the stuff that makes up the object. This law says that the more mass an object has, the greater the force needed to **accelerate** it. To accelerate something means to get it moving or speed it up.

3. For every action there is an equal and opposite reaction. This means for every force or movement, there is an equal force or movement that reacts.

**accelerate** change the speed of a moving object

**inertia** tendency of an object to remain either at rest or in motion unless affected by an outside force

**mass** matter an object contains

Roller coasters follow Newton's laws of motion as they speed around the track.

## THE LEGEND OF SIR ISAAC NEWTON

Isaac Newton isn't just known for describing the laws of motion. He is also known for discovering **gravity**. People tell a famous story about how he made this discovery. The story says that as Newton sat by a tree, he watched an apple fall. Most people wouldn't give this event a second thought. But the falling apple made Newton question what was pulling it straight down instead of in a different direction. His curiosity led to his discovery of the force of gravity.

**gravity** force that pulls objects with mass together; gravity pulls objects down towards the centre of Earth

# CHAPTER 2 INERTIA AT WORK

How does inertia work? You've seen it if you've dropped a ball on a smooth surface. It just keeps rolling. Its motion will change if you grab the ball or it hits something and stops. If left alone, it will eventually slow down and stop. That is because a force called **friction** acts upon the ball as it rolls.

You can find inertia all around at the theme park. Look no further than a roller coaster! Did you know that an engine doesn't power a roller coaster? A cable system with gears pulls it up that first big hill. From there, other forces are at work. The force of gravity pulls it down. Inertia keeps it rolling through more hills and loops. And as it moves, friction between the cars and the track helps it slow down. Eventually, braking force brings the thrilling ride to a full stop.

**friction** force caused by objects rubbing together

You see inertia at work on the Waltzers too. Once your seat gets spinning, it just keeps spinning. Another force can act on the ride to speed up or slow down your spinning. This can happen when the ride changes speed or as you go up and down on the sloped platform. You might even begin spinning in the opposite direction. But to change your spinning motion, there needs to be enough force to resist inertia.

The Waltzer moves along a track as it spins.

## Inertia and the rotor ride

Hop on the rotor ride for another look at inertia. You stand inside a cylindrical room. The room begins spinning. You're spinning around and around. Then, surprise! The floor drops out! But you stay stuck to the wall. Why?

Think about this. Have you ever tied an object to a string and spun it over your head? What happens when you let go? The object keeps moving straight out in the direction it was headed when you let go. That's inertia at work. The string provides a force called centripetal force to keep the object travelling in a circle until you let go.

You are like that object in the rotor ride. This time, it's the walls that keep you from flying off in a straight line. While inertia tries to push you outwards, the walls force you inwards. In fact, their force is so strong that you don't even need the floor to hold you up. When it drops away, you still cling to the wall.

When the bottom drops out, riders stay forced against the wall on the rotor ride.

**centripetal force** force that pulls spinning objects to the centre of a circle

**cylindrical** having a shape with flat, circular ends and sides shaped like a tube

## Inertia at rest

Inertia also keeps things at rest. You can stare all day at that pyramid of bottles at the skittles game. But inertia will keep those bottles where they are. They'll only move when you hit them with the ball you throw at them. *Smash*! The thrown ball applies the force needed to get the bottles moving – and hopefully win you a prize!

Inertia would also let you sit all day at the top of the Ferris wheel if forces didn't act on the ride. Forces come from motors, gravity and other sources. These forces pull and push on the Ferris wheel and many other rides to get them going.

Without forces, you could sit at the top of a Ferris wheel all day.

## Changing direction

Now you've learned two parts of Newton's first law. Objects need forces to get them moving. They also need forces to stop their motion. But there is a third part to Newton's first law. It states that objects need forces to change direction.

Imagine yourself at the very top of a pendulum ride. If you were to drop an object from up there, the force of gravity would pull it straight down to the ground. But when the ride swings downwards, you don't fall straight down. You swing around in a semicircle. Why? It's because the arm attached to your seat changes your direction. It applies centripetal force to keep you travelling in a circular motion.

Inertia would send you flying straight off the roller coaster. But the cars are connected to the track. The design of the track forces you to change direction. It sends you through curves and loops. It doesn't allow your car to go sailing in the direction inertia would send it. It changes your direction.

**pendulum** weight that hangs from a fixed point and swings back and forth freely using the force of gravity

Forces don't need to be directly in contact with something to make them change their direction. When you throw a ball into the air, gravity pulls it down. Gravity acts on the dart you throw in the balloon game too. You need to throw it a bit higher than your target. Why? Gravity begins pulling the dart down as it moves forwards.

Centripetal force acts on the pendulum ride to keep it going in a semicircle.

CHAPTER 3

# THE FORCE OF MOTION

You look in the distance and see a musician carrying a tuba. You also see people carrying big stuffed animals. Which do you think takes more effort to move? The tuba takes more effort (force) to get moving. Newton's second law explains why. This law says that the more mass an object has, the greater the force needed to get it moving (accelerating). The tuba has more mass than the stuffed animal.

A massive Ferris wheel needs a great deal of force to get it going.

You'll see this law at work on the rides too. The more massive the ride, the greater the force needed to get it going and to stop it. It doesn't take much force to get yourself swinging high on a swing because you have a small mass. But a massive Ferris wheel needs the force of big motors to get it going.

**FACT:**

George Washington Gale Ferris Jr built the first Ferris wheel for the World's Fair in 1893. This huge machine weighed 1,300 tonnes. Riders could see 40 kilometres (25 miles) from its 25-storey height.

## F=ma

A simple equation describes Newton's second law: F=ma.

The *F* in the formula stands for force.

The *m* stands for mass.

The *a* stands for acceleration.

The law states that you need a bigger force to get a bigger mass moving. But it works the other way too. Moving objects with more mass will create a more forceful **impact**.

This formula explains why you feel a greater impact when getting slammed into by a large adult in the bumper cars than getting bumped by a small child. You might also see this rule at work at the diving show. A diver with more mass will hit the water with more force – and usually make a bigger splash!

Force, mass and acceleration work together. A change in one will mean that another will also need to change.

---

**impact** forceful contact of objects

The riders on the left can create a more forceful impact than the rider on the right because they have more mass.

## SPEED, VELOCITY AND ACCELERATION

When people talk about motion, they might mention an object's speed, velocity or acceleration. They aren't the same. But they are closely related. Speed tells how fast something is moving. Velocity is similar to speed, but it also tells the direction something is travelling. Acceleration is different. Acceleration is how fast something is speeding up or slowing down. When a car starts from a stop, it's accelerating. Its speed is always changing. Once it gets up to a constant speed, its acceleration is zero.

**FACT:**

The fastest roller coaster in the world is the Formula Rossa in the United Arab Emirates. It has a top speed of 239 kilometres (149 miles) per hour.

## Impact!

Which packs a bigger punch? Getting ploughed into by someone coming full speed off the bottom of the waterslide? Or is the force bigger if you get bumped into by a bumper boat on the lazy river? You've guessed it. The speedy slider will cause the biggest impact because his acceleration is greater. The F=ma formula shows that larger accelerations cause bigger forces.

You'll see how acceleration affects force when you play the carnival games too. What happens when you throw a ball at a stack of bottles? You pull back and throw with all your strength, right? Why? You want to hit the bottles with as much force as you can. The faster you can get the ball going, the more likely you'll knock over the bottles. You need a big force to pack the punch that wins the prize!

Riders speeding down a waterslide can create a forceful impact.

**FACT:**

Did you know that gravity is an acceleration? As objects fall, they speed up. For falling objects the a in the F=ma equation can be replaced with g. The g stands for the acceleration of gravity.

## Momentum

When would it be easier to stop a roller coaster? Would it be when it is halfway down that first death-defying drop? Or would it be easier near the end of the track as it gently rolls down the straight part? That's right. It would take more force to stop the ride at its maximum acceleration. This is because of **momentum**. Momentum depends on an object's mass and velocity. Velocity is a measurement of the speed and direction an object is moving.

Newton's second law explains how momentum works. When an object is accelerating it has momentum. It takes more force to stop something with more acceleration. The faster something is accelerating, the more momentum it gains.

Momentum is at play in many theme park rides. You'll see it in pendulum rides. Momentum is what swings you back up after you swing downwards. Momentum is key to the back and forth swinging of a pendulum. It allows you to keep swinging.

**momentum** amount of force in a moving object determined by the object's mass and velocity

A roller coaster has a great deal of momentum as it speeds down the first hill.

CHAPTER 4

# EQUAL AND OPPOSITE

Now it's time to look for Newton's third law of motion at the park. This law states that for every action there is an equal and opposite reaction. An action is a force that an object **exerts** on something. A reaction is the force that pushes back.

When you ram into another bumper car, you'll notice that both cars bounce back from each other. The action happens when the cars hit. The reaction is when they bounce away. They bounce away from each other with the same amount of force and in opposite directions than they were travelling when they hit. Magnitude describes how big the movement of the cars is.

The lazy river gives us another example of Newton's third law. You get your tube to move forwards by paddling backwards. The action is you pushing the water back. The reaction is your tube moving forwards. The more you push, the more you move forwards.

After two bumper cars hit, they bounce back in the opposite direction.

## THE ENERGY OF IMPACT

Impacts cause more than motion. They also release energy. How do we know? We can hear it and feel it. The crashing noise you hear when two cars hit is energy being released as sound. If you were to touch the bumper on your bumper car after impact, it would feel warm. It feels warm because energy is also released as heat.

**exert** apply

## Where's the equal and opposite reaction?

So what happens when you stomp on the ground? Or flop down on a bench? Your stomping or flopping action doesn't seem to cause a reaction from the ground or the bench. But these objects are reacting. What would happen if they weren't pushing back with an equal and opposite force? Nothing would support your foot or your bottom.

You don't see the ground or the bench react because of their inertia. The action you apply is not enough to get them to change from their states of rest.

You can feel Newton's third law when you push against your strap or bar in a wild ride. The strap is pushing back as hard as you are pushing against it. When do you feel the reaction of your strap most? It's when your action is the greatest, such as when a ride stops suddenly, and your body keeps moving.

As you push against a safety bar, the bar pushes against you.

CHAPTER 5

# ALL TOGETHER NOW!

When you go hurtling down a roller coaster hill, which of Newton's laws are at work? They all are! Newton's laws are acting everywhere all the time. You can combine all the laws to explain a single event.

The force the roller coaster exerts on the track depends on its mass and its acceleration. Also the bigger it is and the more it's accelerating, the greater the force needed to stop it. That's Newton's second law.

When the roller coaster cars push on the track, the track pushes back with an equal force. This force is in the opposite direction. If this were not the case, the track would buckle or the cars would fly off the track. That's Newton's third law.

And what makes the cars sail right up the next hill? That's inertia, part of Newton's first law.

The laws of motion combine for a day of fun at a theme park!

Everywhere you go, all the time – especially at the theme park – the laws of motion are there. Just keep looking, and you'll keep seeing them doing their work!

# GLOSSARY

**accelerate** change the speed of a moving object

**centripetal force** force that pulls spinning objects to the centre of a circle

**cylindrical** having a shape with flat, circular ends and sides shaped like a tube

**exert** apply

**friction** force caused by objects rubbing together

**gravity** force that pulls objects with mass together; gravity pulls objects down towards the centre of Earth

**impact** forceful contact of objects

**inertia** tendency of an object to remain either at rest or in motion unless affected by an outside force

**mass** amount of material in an object

**momentum** amount of force in a moving object determined by the object's mass and velocity

**pendulum** weight that hangs from a fixed point and swings back and forth freely using the force of gravity

**physics** study of matter and energy, including light, heat, electricity and motion

# COMPREHENSION QUESTIONS

1. In the Test your strength game, you hit a pad with a mallet to send a puck up a tower. The higher you send the puck, the higher your strength is rated. Describe how Newton's laws are at work in this game.
2. Explain how F=ma shows that it is easier to push a toy car and get it going than to push a real one.
3. Why do you think you stay in your car when a roller coaster is upside down in a loop? Use reference books or the internet to find information to support your answer.

# FIND OUT MORE

## BOOKS

*Forces and Motion* (Essential Physical Science), Angela Royston (Raintree, 2014)

*Science Experiments: Loads of Explosively Fun Activities You Can Do!,* Robert Winston (DK Children, 2011)

*Zombies and Forces and Motion,* Mark Weakland (Raintree, 2012)

## WEBSITES

**www.bbc.co.uk/bitesize/articles/zywcrdm**
Learn more about the forces that make things move.

**www.dkfindout.com/uk/quiz/science/take-forces-and-motion-quiz**
Take the forces and motion quiz!

# INDEX

science

# COOL PLASTIC BOTTLE SCIENCE

BY TAMMY ENZ

Consultant:
Marcelle A. Siegel
Associate Professor of Science Education
University of Missouri, Missouri, USA

a Capstone company — publishers for children

Raintree is an imprint of Capstone Global Library Limited, a company incorporated in England and Wales having its registered office at 264 Banbury Road, Oxford, OX2 7DY – Registered company number: 6695582

**www.raintree.co.uk**
myorders@raintree.co.uk



Edited by Brenda Haugen
Designed by Russell Griesmer
Picture research by Tracey Cummins
Production by Kathy McColley
Originated by Capstone Press
Printed and bound in China

ISBN 978 1 4747 2197 4
20 19 18 17 16
10 9 8 7 6 5 4 3 2 1

**British Library Cataloguing in Publication Data**
A full catalogue record for this book is available from the British Library.

**Acknowledgements**
We would like to thank the following for permission to reproduce photographs: Capstone Studio: Karon Dubke. Design elements provided by Shutterstock: bimka, FINDEEP, fourb, Golbay, jannoon028, mexrix, Picsfive, Sarunyu_foto, STILLFX, Your Design

# CONTENTS

# COOL PLASTIC BOTTLE SCIENCE

# PLASTIC WITH PURPOSE

Milk, water, juice, pop – it seems like every drink comes in a plastic bottle. When you're done quenching your thirst, where do those bottles go? And where do they come from in the first place? Learn the answers to these questions and more. Then check out exciting ways to repurpose bottles into cool science experiments. Dig into your recycling bin, and get started.

## GREAT PACIFIC GARBAGE PATCH

Plastic bottles are useful and durable. However, if not recycled they often end up in the Great Pacific Garbage Patch. Some scientists think this patch could be six times the size of the UK. Ocean currents trap rubbish dumped on land and in the waters of Asia and North America. Bottles can spend years floating in this rubbish patch, breaking down into tiny pieces called microplastics. Sea animals often mistake plastic pieces for food. Eating plastic can kill them.

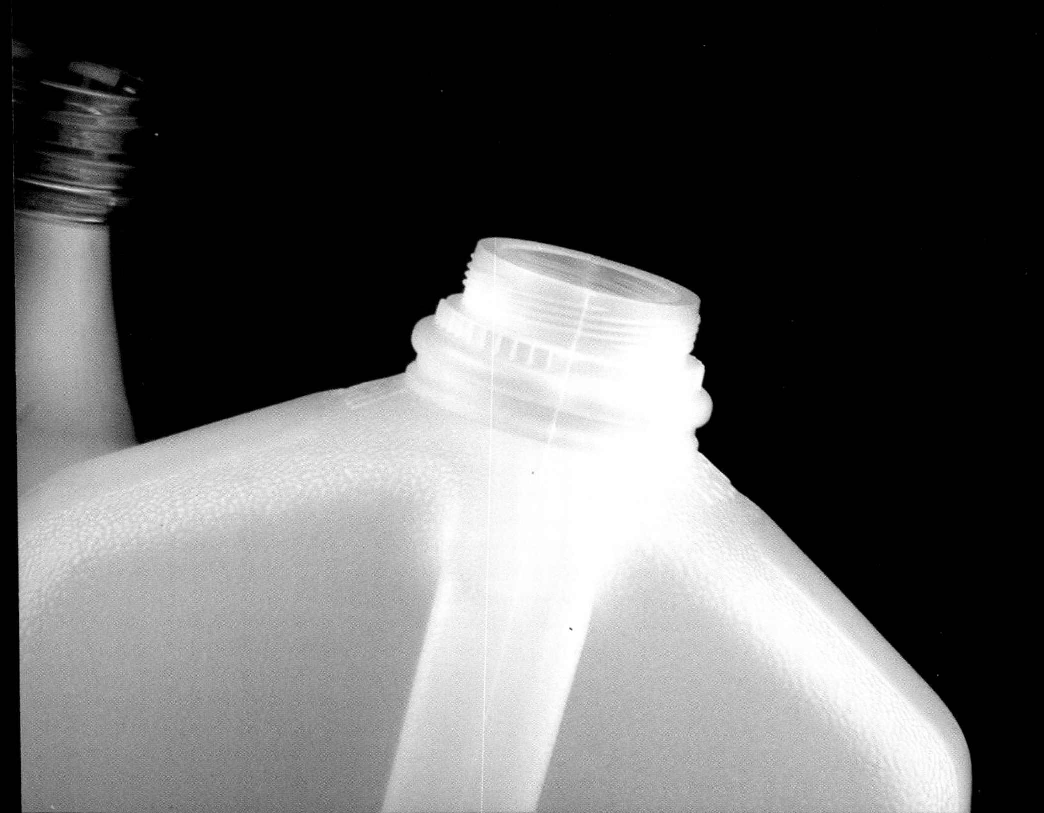

# CLOUD IN A BOTTLE

**Seeing a cloud in the sky might not seem remarkable. But there's a recipe for making clouds. Meet all the conditions, and you can whip one up in your kitchen!**

BRANCH OF SCIENCE: **EARTH SCIENCE**
CONCEPT: **CLOUD FORMATION**

**YOU'LL NEED:**

- Clean, empty 2-litre pop bottle with cap
- Water
- Dark sheet of sugar paper
- Torch
- Matches
- A friend

## PUT IT TOGETHER:

**STEP 1:** Fill the bottom of the bottle with about 2.5 centimetres (1 inch) of water. Screw on the cap. Shake the water around in the bottle.

**STEP 2:** Prop the sugar paper against a wall. Place the bottle in front of it. Squeeze it tightly. Let go.

**STEP 3:** As you let go, ask a friend to shine the torch into the bottle. Do you see a cloud?

STEP 4

**STEP 4:** Ask an adult to light two matches at the same time. Uncap the bottle, and drop the matches in the water. Quickly replace the cap.

**STEP 5:** Shake the bottle, and place it against the paper.

**STEP 6:** Squeeze the bottle tightly, and let it go while a friend shines light on the bottle. For a few seconds you will see a cloud appear.

**STEP 7:** Repeatedly squeeze the bottle to see the cloud form again and again.

## REUSABLE KNOWLEDGE:

By shaking the bottle, you filled it with water vapour. Squeezing the bottle increased the air pressure and the temperature. Releasing the bottle decreased the air pressure and lowered the temperature. Cooling water vapour formed droplets, which clung to the smoke inside. When these three things happen in the atmosphere, clouds form. Dust, smoke or volcanic ash in the air help out.

### FAST FACT:

Bottles and many plastic packages are made from polyethylene terephthalate (PET). PET is a strong lightweight plastic. Its long chains of repeating molecules make it easy to form. Carbon dioxide can't seep through PET, making it ideal for pop bottles.

water vapour  water in its gaseous state

atmosphere  layer of gases surrounding Earth

# MILK BOTTLE SIPHON

**Think you can get water to flow uphill? How about keeping it flowing to drain a bottle dry? You bet. It's easy to do and fun to watch again and again with this experiment.**

BRANCH OF SCIENCE: **EARTH SCIENCE**
CONCEPT: **ATMOSPHERIC PRESSURE**

**YOU'LL NEED:**

- 2 clean, empty milk bottles
- Food colouring (any colour)
- 2.5–3 metres (8–10 feet) clean, clear plastic hose

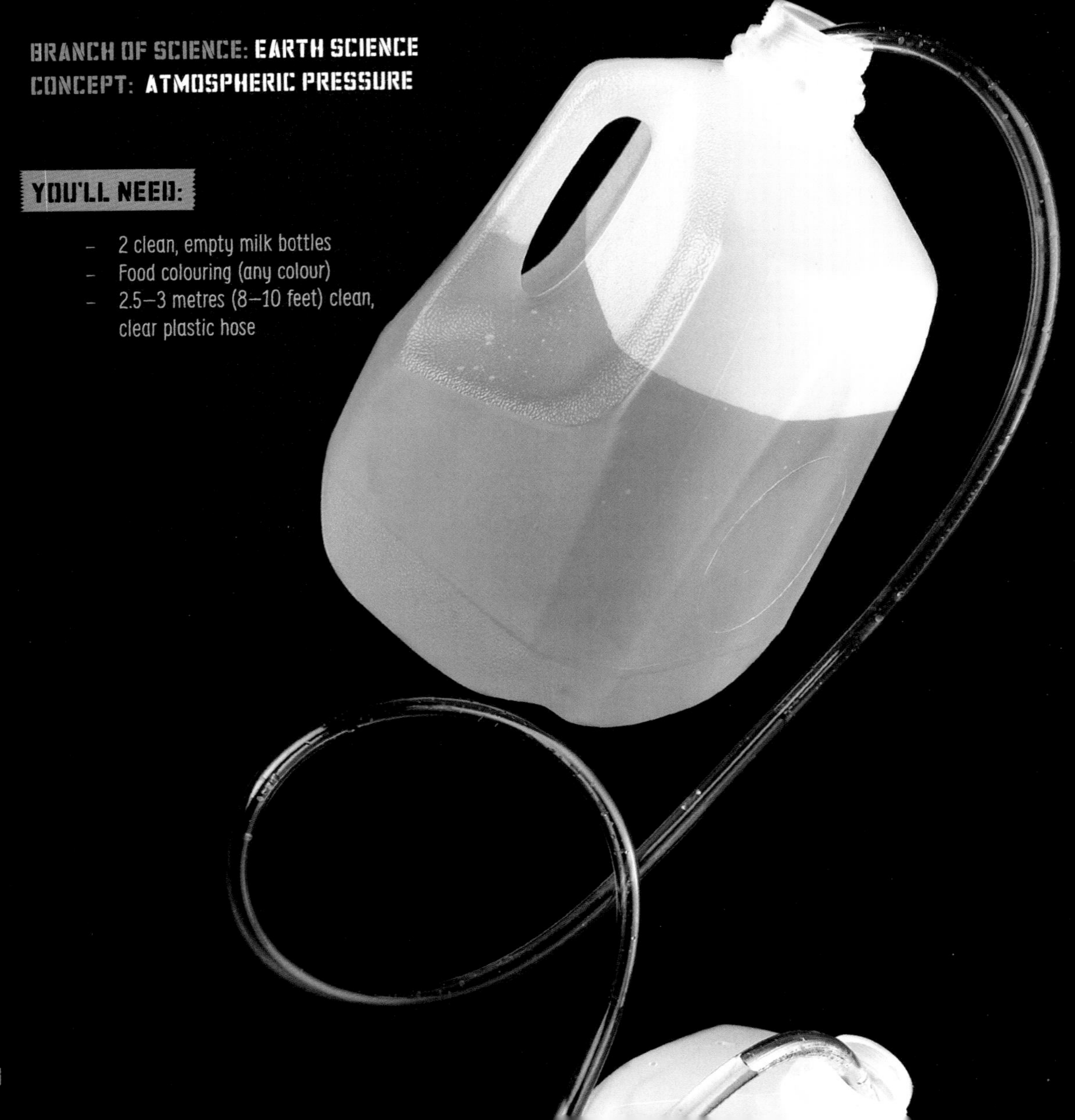

## PUT IT TOGETHER:

**STEP 1:** Fill one bottle with tap water. Add several drops of food colouring.

**STEP 2:** Place this bottle on a table or counter.

**STEP 3:** Place the other bottle on the floor nearby.

**STEP 4:** Insert the hose into the top bottle. Push it all the way in. Make sure its end is near the bottom of the bottle.

**STEP 5:** Place the other end of the hose near the bottom bottle. Include some loops in the hose.

**STEP 6:** Gently suck on the bottom end of the hose. As the water nears your mouth, quickly stick the end inside the bottom bottle. What happens?

STEP 6

## REUSABLE KNOWLEDGE:

Did you realize that the air around you is constantly pushing on you? This pressure is called atmospheric pressure. It's what makes a siphon work. Sucking air out of the tube decreases the pressure inside. This causes atmospheric pressure to push water into the tube. As the water moves through the tube, its pressure is lowered again. Atmospheric pressure keeps pushing until the bottle is dry.

## RECYCLING PLASTIC MILK BOTTLES

Plastic milk bottles are recycled into soap dispensers, garden products and plastic 'wood' planks. 3D printers even use old milk bottles for printing material. Why not use old milk bottles to make more milk bottles? Used bottles could contain impurities, making them unsafe for food packaging.

atmospheric pressure pressure caused by the weight of the atmosphere

# CARTESIAN DIVER

**Your command of this little diver will amaze you. You can thank the properties of gases for this experiment.**

BRANCH OF SCIENCE: **CHEMISTRY**
CONCEPT: **BOYLE'S LAW**

**YOU'LL NEED:**

- Clean, empty 2-litre pop bottle with cap
- Ruler
- Water
- Small sauce packet

## PUT IT TOGETHER:

**STEP 1:** Fill the bottle with water to within 5 centimetres (2 inches) of the top.

**STEP 2:** Drop a sauce packet into the bottle. Make sure it floats just below the water. Experiment with several packets until you find one that works.

**STEP 3:** Screw the cap on the bottle.

**STEP 4:** Squeeze the bottle. What happens?

**STEP 5:** Let it go. What happens now?

## REUSABLE KNOWLEDGE:

An air pocket inside the packet keeps it light enough to float. When you squeeze the bottle, the air pocket becomes smaller. Now the "diver" sinks. This marvel is explained by Boyle's Law. Boyle's Law states that increasing pressure will decrease volume and vice versa.

### FAST FACT:

Water is very heavy. It weighs 1,025 kilograms per cubic metre (64 pounds per cubic foot). The deeper a diver goes under water, the more pressure he feels. Deep-water divers cannot breathe because of the pressure on their lungs. Pressurized air from a SCUBA tank gives lungs enough pressure to combat water pressure. SCUBA stands for Self-Contained Underwater Breathing Apparatus.

# UPSIDE DOWN WATER

**Water can easily flow through a mesh window screen, right? Not so fast! In this experiment water does the unthinkable.**

BRANCH OF SCIENCE: **CHEMISTRY**
CONCEPT: **SURFACE TENSION**

**YOU'LL NEED:**

- Clean, empty milk bottle
- Water
- 15-centimetre (6-inch) square of mesh window screen
- Rubber band
- Several toothpicks
- A friend

## PUT IT TOGETHER:

**STEP 1:** Add water to the bottle until it's 1/3 full.

**STEP 2:** Place the screen over the opening in the bottle. Wrap the rubber band around the screen to hold it to the neck of the milk bottle.

**STEP 3:** Outside or over a sink, carefully turn the bottle upside down. Hold on to the bottle's handle.

**STEP 4:** Steady the bottle while holding the handle. Make sure not to squeeze it. What happens?

**STEP 5:** Ask a friend to carefully push a toothpick through a hole in the screen. What happens?

STEP 2

## REUSABLE KNOWLEDGE:

Water molecules are strongly attracted to one another. This attraction is called cohesion. Under water's surface, molecules are attracted equally in all directions. This attraction is unequal at the water's surface. Here water molecules are attracted inwards only. So molecules act like a thin elastic skin where they meet air. We call this surface tension. This skin stretches across the screen holes. It holds water inside the bottle.

molecule smallest particle of a substance with the properties of that substance

cohesion ability to stick together

surface tension water 'skin'; water molecules form stronger bonds at the surface, causing the surface to act like a membrane

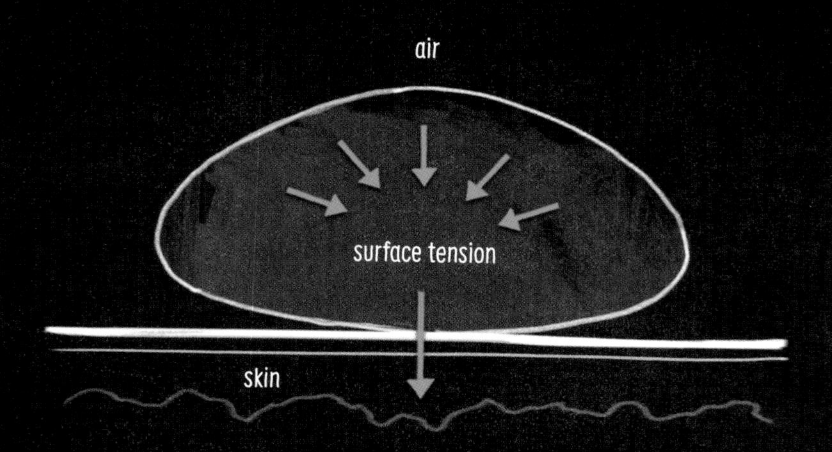


## A WATERY SKIN

Surface tension acts like a skin on water's surface. Small drops of liquid are spherical because cohesion pulls the molecules inwards.

# BALLOON INFLATOR

**Blowing up balloons can wear out your lungs. Get something else do the work. A little chemical reaction is all it takes.**

BRANCH OF SCIENCE: **CHEMISTRY**
CONCEPT: **ACID/BASE REACTION**

**YOU'LL NEED:**

- Balloon (not inflated)
- Funnel
- 38 grams (1/8 cup) bicarbonate of soda
- Clean, empty pop bottle, 0.6 litres (20 ounces) or smaller
- Vinegar

## PUT IT TOGETHER:

**STEP 1:** Place the tip of the funnel inside the balloon.

**STEP 2:** Pour the bicarbonate of soda into the funnel. Shake the bicarbonate of soda into the balloon.

**STEP 3:** Add vinegar to the bottle until it's about half full.

**STEP 4:** Remove the funnel. Stretch the neck of the balloon over the top of the bottle. Make sure none of the bicarbonate of soda falls into the vinegar.

**STEP 5:** Hold the neck of the balloon tightly to the bottle. Tip the balloon to dump the bicarbonate of soda into the vinegar. What happens?

## REUSABLE KNOWLEDGE:

Vinegar is an acid, and bicarbonate of soda is a base. Acids and bases react to make a new product. In this case, carbon dioxide gas is made. You can't always see a gas, but in this experiment the gas is easy to detect. It expands to fill the balloon. If you've ever made a cake, you've seen an acid and base reaction. Bubbles from reacting ingredients make the cake light and fluffy.

## RECYCLING POP BOTTLES

Think you'd look good wearing pop bottles? How about using them to decorate your home? That's exactly where most recycled PET ends up. It is processed into many new materials including carpet fibre, T-shirt fabric, shoes and luggage. It is also used to make new PET containers for food and non-food products.

acid sour tasting substance that reacts with a base

base bitter tasting substance that reacts with an acid

# VINEGAR ROCKET

A blasting rocket is an exciting experiment. This rocket uses things you find around your house. It packs a punch and explains an important physics law.

YOU'LL NEED:

- Clean, empty pop bottle
- Vinegar
- 7 grams (1 teaspoon) of bicarbonate of soda
- 1 square of toilet tissue
- Tape
- Cardboard hot chocolate canister (must be wide enough for the pop bottle to fit into)
- Cork that fits snugly in the mouth of the pop bottle

BRANCH OF SCIENCE: **PHYSICS**
CONCEPT: **NEWTON'S THIRD LAW OF MOTION**

## PUT IT TOGETHER:

**STEP 1:** Add vinegar to the bottle until it's 3/4 full. Put it aside.

**STEP 2:** Place the bicarbonate of soda in the centre of the toilet tissue. Carefully roll the tissue into a tight tube around the bicarbonate of soda.

**STEP 3:** Fold the ends over, and tape them in place to make a small packet. Make sure the packet is small enough to fit inside the mouth of the pop bottle.

**STEP 4:** Find an open area outside. Place the cardboard canister on the ground or prop it at an angle with bricks or rocks. Make sure the canister is not pointing towards people, animals or windows.

**STEP 5:** Drop the packet into the bottle. Quickly cork it. Put it cork side down inside the canister.

**STEP 6:** Back up several metres, and wait. It may take a little while for the rocket to take off. Do not go near it as you wait!

**STEP 7:** Find the landing place of your rocket.
Then do the experiment again!

STEP 2

STEP 5

## REUSABLE KNOWLEDGE:

This experiment shows Newton's Third Law of Motion. This law states that for every action there is an equal and opposite reaction. The vinegar and bicarbonate of soda reaction forms carbon dioxide. The carbon dioxide explodes backwards from the bottle. An equal force pushes the bottle forwards. This is the same principle that lifts rockets into space.

# SUB IRRIGATED PLANTER

**Do you like gardening? Are you sometimes afraid of watering your plants too little or too much? Try this project. It uses an important biology concept to keep plants watered just right.**

BRANCH OF SCIENCE: **BIOLOGY**
CONCEPT: **CAPILLARY ACTION**

## YOU'LL NEED:

- Clean, empty 2-litre bottle
- Ruler
- Marker pen
- Utility knife
- 3 strips of cotton from an old T-shirt, 2.5 centimetres wide x 10 centimetres (1 inch x 4 inches) long
- 700 grams (3 cups) potting soil
- Lettuce or herb seeds
- Water

## SAFETY FIRST:

Ask an adult to help when using sharp tools such as a utility knife.

**STEP 1:** Make a mark 8 centimetres (3 inches) from the top of the bottle. Use the utility knife to cut a small "x" at this spot.

**STEP 2:** Repeat Step 1 to make a total of six small x's. Make them evenly spaced around the bottle 8 centimetres (3 inches) from the top.

**STEP 3:** Use the utility knife to cut off the top half of the bottle.

**STEP 4:** Turn the top upside down, and place it inside the bottom half.

**STEP 5:** Lay the fabric strips inside the top part of the bottle. They should extend through the neck of the bottle and touch the bottle's bottom.

**STEP 6:** Pack the soil around the cotton strips.

**STEP 7:** Plant seeds in the soil according to the package directions. Lightly water the seeds from the top.

**STEP 8:** Lift the top, and pour several centimetres of water into the bottle bottom. Replace the top.

**STEP 9:** Wait for your seeds to sprout and grow. Refill the bottom with water as needed.

## REUSABLE KNOWLEDGE:

Like a straw, plant cells draw water and minerals upwards. This upward flow is called capillary action. Your waterer also uses capillary action. Water moves through openings in the cotton and soil to reach the plant's roots.

capillary action  ability of liquid to flow in small places against the force of gravity

# LAVA LAMP

A lava lamp gives off a one-of-a-kind glow. Its dancing blobs bring hours of enjoyment. Make your own with this project. Then pride yourself on knowing the science behind it.

BRANCH OF SCIENCE: **CHEMISTRY**
CONCEPT: **OIL AND WATER IMMISCIBILITY**

**YOU'LL NEED:**

- Clean, empty pop or water bottle (any size)
- Water
- Vegetable oil
- Food colouring (any colour)
- Effervescent tablets (Alka-Seltzer)
- Battery-operated tea light

## PUT IT TOGETHER:

**STEP 1:** Add water to the bottle until it's 1/4 full.

**STEP 2:** Pour vegetable oil into the bottle until it is nearly full.

**STEP 3:** Drop 6 to 10 drops of food colouring into the bottle. Shake the bottle if needed to dissolve the food colouring.

**STEP 4:** Wait until the water and oil have separated. Place 1/4 of an effervescent tablet into the bottle. Watch the show!

**STEP 5:** When the bubbles stop, place another 1/4 tablet into the bottle. This time place the lit tea light upside down in the top of the bottle.

**STEP 6:** Take the lamp into a dark room for a lava lamp experience.

**STEP 7:** Add more tablets, 1/4 at a time, to keep the fun going.

STEP 4

## REUSABLE KNOWLEDGE:

The oil and water don't mix together. Why? Water is much more dense than oil. Its molecules are more tightly packed together than oil's are. This makes water sink. The structure of the molecules is different for oil and water too. Water's molecules are polar, meaning they have a negative charge on one end and a positive charge on the other. Their charges hold the molecules to each other. Oil is nonpolar, without a charge, and doesn't mingle with the water molecules. The fizzing tablet releases gas. As the gas rises to the surface, it pulls coloured water with it. After the gas escapes, the water blobs sink back to the bottom of the bottle.

polar molecule with one slightly positively charged and one slightly negatively charged end

nonpolar uncharged molecule

# COMPOSTING WORM FARM

Recycle more than a pop bottle with this project. Recycle your kitchen scraps too. This project does more than keep rubbish out of a landfill. It improves the environment!

BRANCH OF SCIENCE: **BIOLOGY**
CONCEPT: **SOIL SCIENCE**

## YOU'LL NEED:

- Clean, empty 2-litre bottle
- Utility knife
- 0.5-litre (16.9-ounce) water bottle filled with room temperature water
- Small scoop
- Ruler
- Sand
- Soil
- Fruit and vegetable peelings
- 0.12 litres (1/2 cup) of water
- 3 or 4 earthworms

## SAFETY FIRST:

Ask an adult to help when using sharp tools such as a utility knife.

## PUT IT TOGETHER:

**STEP 1:** Use the utility knife to cut the top off the 2-litre bottle. Cut it where the bottle starts to get narrower near the top. Discard the top.

**STEP 2:** Place the water bottle centred inside the 2-litre bottle. This will keep the worms near the outside of the bottle so you can watch them.

**STEP 3:** Carefully scoop about 2.5 centimetres (1 inch) of sand into the larger bottle. Make sure the water bottle stays in place.

**STEP 4:** Add about 2.5 centimetres (1 inch) of soil.

**STEP 5:** Add a layer of fruit and vegetable peelings.

**STEP 6:** Continue layering 2.5-centimetres (1-inch) layers of sand, soil and peelings. Stop when you reach about 5 centimetres (2 inches) from the top of the bottle.

**STEP 7:** Slowly pour water over the layers to make them slightly damp.

**STEP 8:** Add the worms.

**STEP 9:** Place the bottle in a cool, dark place.

**STEP 10:** Add small amounts of water every couple of days to keep the worm farm moist. Watch daily until the worms have composted all the scraps.

**STEP 11:** After several weeks, pour the newly composted soil and worms into a planter or flowerbed. Let them continue their work.

## REUSABLE KNOWLEDGE:

Worms are nature's great recyclers. Worms turn food scraps and dead plants into rich soil fertilizer. As worms eat, their bodies change scraps into compost. They poop out this fertilizer to keep plants strong and healthy. Test out how well fertilizer works. Do plants grow better in composted soil or regular soil?

compost breaks down fruits, vegetables and other materials to make soil better for gardening

# GLOSSARY

**acid** sour tasting substance that reacts with a base

**atmosphere** layer of gases surrounding Earth

**atmospheric pressure** pressure caused by the weight of the atmosphere

**base** bitter tasting substance that reacts with an acid

**capillary action** ability of liquid to flow in small places against the force of gravity

**cohesion** ability to stick together

**compost** breaks down fruits, vegetables and other materials to make soil better for gardening

**molecule** smallest particle of a substance with the properties of that substance

**nonpolar** uncharged molecule

**polar** molecule with one slightly positively charged and one slightly negatively charged end

**surface tension** water 'skin'; water molecules form stronger bonds at the surface, causing the surface to act like a membrane

**water vapour** water in its gaseous state

## READ MORE

*101 Great Science Experiments*, Neil Ardley (DK Children, 2015)

*365 Science Activities*, Various (Usborne Publishing, 2014)

*Big Book of Science Things to Make and Do*, Rebecca Gilpin and Leonie Pratt (Usborne Publishing, 2012)

*Really Rotten Experiments (Horrible Science)*, Nick Arnold (Scholastic, 2014)

## WEBSITES

**www.bbc.co.uk/education/clips/zhbygk7**
Does gas weigh anything? Find out in this video from BBC Bitesize.

**www.bbc.co.uk/education/clips/zdhxpv4**
Watch this video to see a homemade water rocket in action!

**www.rigb.org/families/experimental**
This website has lots of videos showing fun experiments you can do at home.

## COMPREHENSION QUESTIONS

1. Describe the two concepts that cause bubbles to rise and drop back in the lava lamp project on p. 24.

2. Water is held inside an upside down bottle with a mesh window screen on p. 12. What term describes water's ability to do this?

3. Describe how a bottle dropped in a California, USA river might make its way to the Great Pacific Garbage Patch?

# INDEX